The quiet calling

Jeannie Lymath

Presentation by *BookLeaf Publishing*

Web: www.bookleafpub.com

E-mail: info@bookleafpub.com

ISBN: 9789357695756

First edition 2022

This book is dedicated to my biggest believer....my Mum.

ACKNOWLEDGEMENT

Thank you to my children, my greatest achievements and the most brutal teachers, all those incredibly deep conversations that have inspired so many dreams. I hope this helps you see that anything is possible.

To Scott who has always let me run free with dreams and emotions, being that solid rock every single day and helping me see through the endless thoughts that live inside my brain.

To my soul sisters, brothers and family who have always supported my journey, teaching me to be true to myself and opening up new experiences to live a bigger life that I ever intended.

And to my Daddy who let me read his raw poems and gave me a love of words.

PREFACE

I have been obsessed with reading my entire life, often found in a quiet corner snuggled with a book. My daddy wrote poems, I thought he was so talented, and although his dream faded it lit a flame within me. This is a celebration of all the inspiring words I have read, listened to with my whole heart and weaved into being.

Can you feel it?

Can you feel the beating of the drum?

    the faint vibration moving through forests &
mountains,
                making your body tingle &
your heart skip a beat.

Can you feel the beating of the drum?

    the ancestral call that tugs lightly on your
being,
                awakening a fire that resides
within you.

Can you feel the beating of the drum?

    the pull to walk the beaten path that was
carved before,
                and recall the unheard stories
of their souls.

Can you feel the beating of the drum?

    that roars through your blood & swirls
unbounding you,

rising anger & silent screams
unleashed.

Can you feel the beating of the drum?

the whisper of secrets that beckons on the
wind,
quietly enveloping you as each
step gets bolder.

Grandmother Moon

I catch the wink of the Moon reminding me to
breathe & take a moment longer,
keep believing
my child
she says.

I catch the silvery glow of the Moon bathing me
in hope & wonder,
celebrate now
my child
she says.

I catch the slither of the Moon guiding me
towards places unknown,
reflect now
my child
she says.

I catch the darkness of the Moon still bright in
my heart but abandoned in the sky,
stay still now
my child
she says.

No more

That tickle became a cough that she hoped
would go,
 but it grew & grew until there was only silence
in pain,
  shackles tightened until there was no light at
all,
    silence met by screams that roared louder
within,
    memories from beyond tore her soul as the
anger arose,
no,
  no,
    no,
     no,
      no,
words brandished her mind,
                no more,
                  no more,
days passed before she awoke
                  and the burning
had gone,
the cough returned back to a tickle
                  and then no
more,

a woman was reborn with boundaries and power,
 and the pain from the past was no longer an
enemy,
   but a teacher to remind her of the words
      no more.

Sacred Flame

The sacred flame may flicker but ne'er dies,
wave after wave of emotional transformation,
never afraid of the thousand eyes,
looking upon the road of creativity,
exploring life's burning spotlight,
hissing and sparking anguish,
shimmering and flaring with pleasure,
entwined with a silvery intuition,
My power,
My pleasure,
My pain.

Time

silvery wings of flight are hovering, waiting
patiently,
 fluttering before my eyes,
  subtle like the rainbow through the window,
   the colours fading with time.

  as the time blurs and melts in front of me,
  the ever-knowing constriction torments my
heart,
 i collect the words of love as trinkets to wear,
sparkling with desperation that taints the vitality.

watching the vibrancy of life transform,
 hoping that the wings keep the fire from dying,
  shepherding quiet exhales to keep the embers
alive,
  another moment of maternal touch so exquisite
that I cry.

  time
  waits
 for
no one.

Dreams

my
heart
bleeds for
the perpetual suffering,
perpetual stagnant change rising,
the iron fist controlling,
fighting harder ever desperate to win.

will
the
battle
ever
end?
so my soul can rest once more,
waters returning with clear clarity,
forests teeming with life,
where the land belongs to no one at all.

I
dream
of
that
place
in
time,

but will man still be standing?
vines will hide the destruction,
nature unattended magnificently,
fear no more children, the trees will be your
friend.

The dancer of joy

twirling
 i burst forth with an unbridled fountain of joy
  a wild abandon as I spin and spin endlessly

spinning
 a trail of delightful hope on the stage of life
  undulating awareness into being stretching
beyond

clapping
 i touch the darkness with sounds of truth
  arms stretching tendrils of illumination into the
shadow

watching
 as the passion ignites a wave of ecstasy
  transforming everything it touches to gold

alchemy
 the eternal reshaping of happiness from the
doom and gloom
  movement of joyful magic, I am the dancer of
joy

Lemuria

the song of the dolphins enters my soul
  unlocking the cobweb of hidden memories
    glistening tendrils draw me closer to the
temples
      an awareness bursting through my heart
so incredibly hot
        like molten lava it engulfs me
        transforming as it burns
        waves of cooling turquoise caressing my
body
      melodies entwining with flickers of dreams
  heightened consciousness aflame with emotion
bringing me back to Lemuria, my homeland, the
land of Mu

Little Monkey

hey
little monkey
won't you show me the way
take me dancing, take me leaping,
laughing mischievously, instead of hiding away.

hey
little monkey
are you sure this is the way
to live carefree, to jump in the puddles,
unleashing the naughtiness, instead of locking
the wild inside.

hey
little monkey
why did i hide you away
attempting perfection, to be loved,
thinking you were bad, instead little monkey you
are free.

Tapping

tap
tap
tap
tap
tapping on my windowpane
pounding rain against my mind
torrential drips that soak my soul
doubt whistling away
drowning out the light
sludge poisons my blood
and slows my body
stuck in the mud
sinking slowly with emotion
the only sound
tap
tap
tap
tap

Are you sure?

are
you
sure?
I mean, it hasn't been done before

are
you
sure?
I mean, are you good enough

are
you
sure?
I mean, what if it doesn't work

are
you
sure?
I mean, you cannot possibly know

are
you
sure?
I mean, what if it all goes wrong

are
you
sure?
I mean, you will probably fail

are
you
sure?
I mean, you may not be strong

are
you
sure?

Enough

Am I enough
    to fit in with that faded picture
        that has cracked over time
            from a lack of care.

Am I enough
    to stand shoulder to shoulder
        now that your back has withered
            and you can no longer look down.

Am I enough
    to express myself freely
        unrestrained steps
            safely surrounded by darkness.

Am I enough
    to be seen clearly
        without the thread of hormones
            steering my screaming mind to be
ignored.

Am I enough
    to have a seat at the table
        holding those past screams in my
lap

                    honouring them without
hysteria.

Am I enough
        yes I am
                but are you?

Power

Your words have power
 I am
  I will
   I can
    I have
     At ease
      Effortless
       I receive
        I believe
         I achieve
You do not have to wish for the impossible someday,
Fill your cauldron with dreams and stir in that action,
Allow the intentions to simmer and boil,
And drink that elixir of transformation.

The High Priestess

Sitting at the threshold of the unconscious mind,
The thin veil of awareness flutters in the breeze,
Hidden mysteries awaiting to be revealed,
As the duality of darkness and light always
prevails,
Balancing energies with majestic ease,
Inviting intuition proudly whilst sat on the
throne,
Unveiling inner wisdom silently so sure,
Tapping her fingers upon the scrolls of power,
Under the moonlight wondering whether to
show more,
Have you earnt access to the portal of trust?
Or will you be left waiting, wanting more?

Venus

Born with a painful fury that can only be
extinguished with ecstasy
Your search is never ending as you glimpse the
flame beyond the veil
Unfailingly out of reach through timeless
centuries and lifetimes
Clay and mud clings to your skin as
you heave through hell
To discover your twin flame, a
quest for your dark soul
A serpent of pleasure uncoiling, secretly
unfolding your destiny
As the essence of Venus pulsates deep
through your veins
Incarnating an eternal yearning
of obsessed passion
Where emotions cannot be distinguished from
your heart's desires
Step by step you hypnotically sniff out this
infuriating intoxication
So that you can find the bright light
that thrives upon yours
More fevered, more passionate, without
any maddening reason

This intoxicating Venus
governing your confusion
You want everything slithering
slowly, but nothing at all
You want everything,
hissing furiously for more
Venus silently
writhing within your soul

Spinning

A circle of doubt
Is it me or you?
Eyes just like mine
Hoping for questions to be answered
In this confusing society
Where I still don't know
If I fit in?
Am loved?
Or even accepted as me....
What step do I take?
What action do I need?
This circle of doubt
Spinning around me

Crystalline

Intermingling energy colliding in the darkness
   Born with the volcanic pressure of the
mysterious
   Slowly dripping with the consciousness of
minerals
      Bursting with knowledge of bygone folklore
       The infinity patterns supporting the magical
incessantly
         As the crystalline power whispers secret
intentions
           Encouraging rainbows of enlightenment
            Love transforming the stagnant souls
             The higher vibrations alluring celestial
creations
              Unfurling frightened wings to soar in
the heavens
               Crystalline momentum opening
your eyes to the purpose
                A life-long understanding of the
perpetual flame
                 Residing within you, governing
your heart and your soul

Emotion

Stepping toe first into watery emotion
The lapping waves tentatively cleansing my
body
Moving further inward as I swim into the
darker depths
A cold enveloping me, confessing my
anger to the ocean
Discarding my mask of illusion, the deeper I
tread
Waves encircling my mind with undines
emerging
Conductors of my emotional pollution
Cosmic currents resounding through the water
My unloving speech swiftly transforming
The anxiety unwrapping from my heart
Allowing abuse and indulgence to dissolve
Precipitating glorious forgiveness upon my
forehead
A kiss from sea as my subconscious renews

Drummers

when the women were drummers
the
beat
perpetuated the circle of life
creating warrior hearts
        that fiercely protected
driving hunters
        to eradicate lonely hunger
the
beat
created medicine
        bringing harmony to bodies
dancing in celebration
        of their dear life
a beautiful balance
        of nature and need
the
beat
reminded them of the past
        the battles of ancestors
sensitive to the power
        beholden to them
the elixir of reverence
        at the wonder of the land
the

beat
reminding them of their duty
        to their blissful existence
to themselves, their families,
        their lovers, their community
Keeping this land thriving
        with life beyond just them

Little Sister

Oh, little sister won't you take my hand
     forget about the thoughts of others for
today
        let's be silly with creativity weaving
our own magic
          and laugh chaotically, spinning
wildly.

Oh, little sister won't you skip with me
     unleash that well-hidden hurt inner child
       let it be free like your hair on the
breeze
        giggling uncontrollably as we
sing flamboyantly.

Oh, little sister won't you run in the sea with me
     unburdening your frustrations to the water
       as we splash among the untamed
waves
        and play as we used to, so simply
carefree.

Oh, little sister won't you pick flowers with me
     garlands of daisy chains adorning your
body

buttercups reflecting your bright light
within you
                grounding your soul deeply,
unbound and free to fly.

Brigid

Enflamed heart of compassion
    heats the sufferers' endless aches
Mother medicine of healing
    Soothes the souls of the broken hearted
Warrior hammers of iron
    Forged to defend the weakened populace
Brigid stands in her emboldened power
    ready to help the armies of lost players

Twisting and turning as every need arises
    weaving a faith for the droves of helpless
No stranger refused at the threshold of hope
    after miles of blisters and bitter desperation
All folk considered worthy of simple love
    upholding her sanctuary with acts of
devotion
Brigid is the beacon of selfless duty
    the braiding of three keeping the flame
eternal